Where did they come from...

DINOSAURS

...and where did they go?

Where did they come from...
DINOSAURS
...and where did they go?

Elaine Graham-Kennedy, Ph.D.
Foreword by **Jerry D. Thomas**

Pacific Press® Publishing Association
Nampa, Idaho
Oshawa, Ontario, Canada
www.pacificpress.com

Book design and illustrations by Gerald Lee Monks
Cover photo of *Velociraptor* courtesy of Geoscience Research Institute, Loma Linda, California
Photos by dreamstime.com and iStockphoto.com

Additional copies of this book are available by
calling toll free 1-800-765-6955
or by visiting <AdventistBookCenter.com>.

ISBN 13: 978-0-8163-2155-1
ISBN 10: 0-8163-2155-8

06 07 08 09 10 • 5 4 3 2 1

This book is dedicated to
my granddaughter, Mikayla,
a *very* curious young lady.

CONTENTS

FOREWORD

Kids love dinosaurs. There's no escaping it. Their curiosity about those exotic creatures—large and small—seems to know no end. But for the most part, their sources of information about dinosaurs have been mired deep in the teachings of evolution and a world without God.

That's why I'm so glad to see this book come into print. Here parents and teachers will find scientific facts explained in words kids can understand. More importantly, they'll find scientific facts explained by someone who believes in God and in the Bible's account of Creation.

Too many of us were taught that dinosaurs never really lived, that the fossil skeletons were the result of combining the skeletons of multiple animals. It's time to face the facts head on and try to figure out where dinosaurs once fit into God's creation.

There is a great deal that science doesn't know or understand about dinosaurs. Much of what is portrayed in books, movies, and television about their appearance and behavior is simply speculation. I appreciate that in this book, Dr. Kennedy doesn't speculate. She draws a careful line between what is known and what people imagine might be true.

Rather than tell us what to believe about dinosaurs, Dr. Kennedy lays out the facts that are known and invites us to think things through for ourselves. This, I believe, is an excellent teaching technique for kids. When we give them a solid basis of facts and faith to build on, they are free to let their imagination soar in a world where dinosaurs roam and God rules.

Jerry D. Thomas

Dinosaur Lover and Hunter

WHEN I WAS A GIRL, I loved dinosaurs. I talked my mom into buying a certain kind of cereal because if you collected ten box tops, you could mail them in and get a small plastic dinosaur. My mom is so great! She kept buying that cereal, and I ate it all just to get a *Stegosaurus*, a *Triceratops*, and a *Brontosaurus*. (If you don't know how to pronounce the names of the dinosaurs in this book, look them up on page 80.) I never did get a T-rex. I probably got tired of eating that cereal.

I loved those little plastic dinosaurs, and I played with them a lot. I don't know what happened to them. I think my brother used them as targets for his army set.

My favorite dinosaur in those days was the *Stegosaurus*, the one with two full rows of plates down its back and spikes on its tail. Scientists didn't think it was very smart, so I was sure it would follow me everywhere—just like a puppy! Today I have a very colorful little model *Stegosaurus* that walks by itself.

My *Triceratops* had short horns and a small frill on the back of its head. It was very different from the purple one I have now, which has long horns and a large, spiked frill. You probably know already that all the colors are fakes. That's because no one really knows what color the skin of dinosaurs was. Too bad! They probably were pretty animals.

At the time I got my first collection of toy dinosaurs, the models looked exactly like what paleontologists (dinosaur scientists) thought the real animals looked like when they were alive. Things have changed a lot since then!

The saddest change of all is the loss of the name *Brontosaurus*. It was such a great name! Someone made the first *Brontosaurus* skeleton by putting a *Camarasaurus* head on an *Apatosaurus* body. When scientists discovered the mistake, the name *Brontosaurus* had to go. I told some people about this one time, and a man got really upset with me. *Brontosaurus* was his favorite dinosaur!

We know more about dinosaurs than ever before, but there is still a lot to learn. That's why I've spent years digging in the dirt around dinosaur bones and eggs. (I was really amazed when I learned people will pay you to dig in the dirt!) Sometimes the weather has been extremely hot and dry; other times it's been so rainy we couldn't work. We didn't care; we just enjoyed learning more and more about dinosaurs.

I want to tell you some of the things I've learned about these incredible animals that God created. Let's go looking for dinosaurs—or at least for what we can learn about them.

Photos courtesy Elaine Graham-Kennedy.

JUST A FEW MORE FRIENDS
IN MY TOY DINOSAUR COLLECTION.

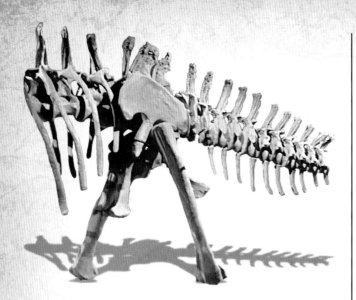

FIGURE 2.1. The reptilelike hip structure and quadrupedal nature of *Diplodocus* places these dinosaurs in the saurischian group. (Quadrupeds walk on four feet.) The general term for these dinosaurs is sauropod. *Photo courtesy Timothy G. Standish and the North American Museum of Ancient Life.*

FIGURE 2.2. *Coelophysis* was also a saurischian, but it was bipedal (walks on two feet) and carnivorous (meateating). We call these animals theropods. *Photo courtesy Natural History Museum of Los Angeles County.*

TO BEGIN OUR HUNT for dinosaurs, we need to know some basic facts about their bones. Once we know a little about the bones, we can figure out which dinosaur we've found. But first, since dinosaur names can be pretty confusing, I'll explain them.

You can see that some dinosaur names are in italic type, which looks like *this*. The names written in italics are the formal names used by scientists. *Triceratops* is an example of a formal name that most people seem to know. Formal names are in a language called Latin. I don't think scientists use much imagination when they name things. If they didn't have the Latin language to help them, the plant and animal names would be pretty boring.

The formal name of the most famous of all saurischian theropods is *Tyrannosaurus rex*. But most people don't want to take the time to say *Tyrannosaurus rex*. They want to use a name that's easy to say and easy to remember, like T-rex. That's called the common name. The letters in the common name are not written in italics. (A list on page 80 of this book tells you how to pronounce dinosaur names and a few other important words.)

DINOSAUR HIPS

Scientists sort the dinosaurs they find into groups that have similar skeletons. Let's start with a quick look at the hips of the dinosaurs.

Scientists classify all dinosaurs by the way their hipbones are shaped.

FIGURE 2.3. View of a kid's hip. *Photo courtesy Dreamstime.com*

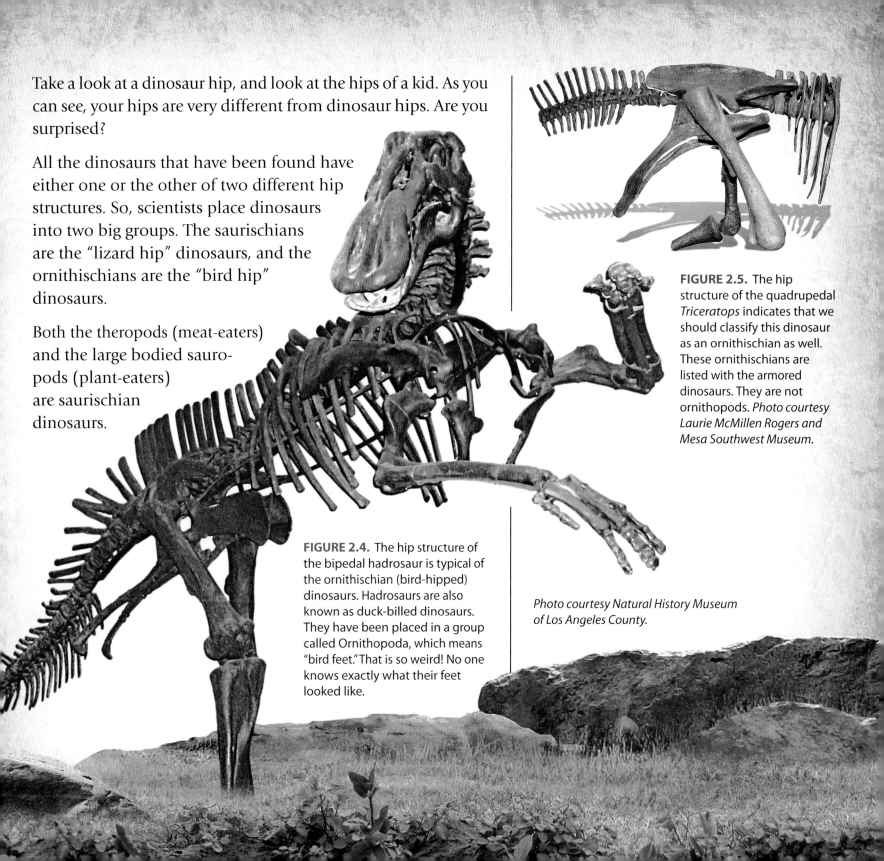

Take a look at a dinosaur hip, and look at the hips of a kid. As you can see, your hips are very different from dinosaur hips. Are you surprised?

All the dinosaurs that have been found have either one or the other of two different hip structures. So, scientists place dinosaurs into two big groups. The saurischians are the "lizard hip" dinosaurs, and the ornithischians are the "bird hip" dinosaurs.

Both the theropods (meat-eaters) and the large bodied sauropods (plant-eaters) are saurischian dinosaurs.

FIGURE 2.5. The hip structure of the quadrupedal *Triceratops* indicates that we should classify this dinosaur as an ornithischian as well. These ornithischians are listed with the armored dinosaurs. They are not ornithopods. *Photo courtesy Laurie McMillen Rogers and Mesa Southwest Museum.*

FIGURE 2.4. The hip structure of the bipedal hadrosaur is typical of the ornithischian (bird-hipped) dinosaurs. Hadrosaurs are also known as duck-billed dinosaurs. They have been placed in a group called Ornithopoda, which means "bird feet." That is so weird! No one knows exactly what their feet looked like.

Photo courtesy Natural History Museum of Los Angeles County.

Did you know that most of the people who read and write about dinosaurs know more about dinosaurs than they know about God? That's terrible! If we're going to talk with those people about dinosaurs, we need to know the basic facts. When they see that we know about dinosaurs too, they might listen when we talk about the God who created them. It's important to be able to talk with people about things they love and the God you love. That's why I study dinosaurs —to tell people about God's love.

Many Christians ask, "Where did the dinosaurs come from? How did the dinosaur bones get here?" They want to know how dinosaurs fit into what the Bible says about this earth's history. We need to be able to talk to them about dinosaurs and God too.

By looking at the photos of the *Diplodocus* and *Coelophysis*, you can see that their hips have basically the same shape.

The second major group is the ornithischian dinosaurs. The hipbones of these dinosaurs were similar to birds' hipbones. Some of these dinosaurs walked on two feet, but many of them walked on four feet. All of the ornithischian dinosaurs ate plants.

There are two groups of ornithischian dinosaurs. The first group is the ornithopods. The name means "bird foot," and the tracks of these dinosaurs look like bird tracks. When feeding, they probably used all four feet. Lots of ornithischian dinosaurs are listed as ornithopods. The hadrosaurs and lambeosaurs are "duck bill" dinosaurs. Both of them are ornithischian ornithopods.

The second group of ornithischian dinosaurs has large, hard plates and spikes on their heads, bodies, and tails. The spikes and plates look like armor, so scientists call these dinosaurs the "armored" dinosaurs. The *Triceratops* is one of these dinosaurs. Check out its hips (figure 2-5)! Both ornithopods and armored dinosaurs have birdlike hips, so all of them are ornithischians.

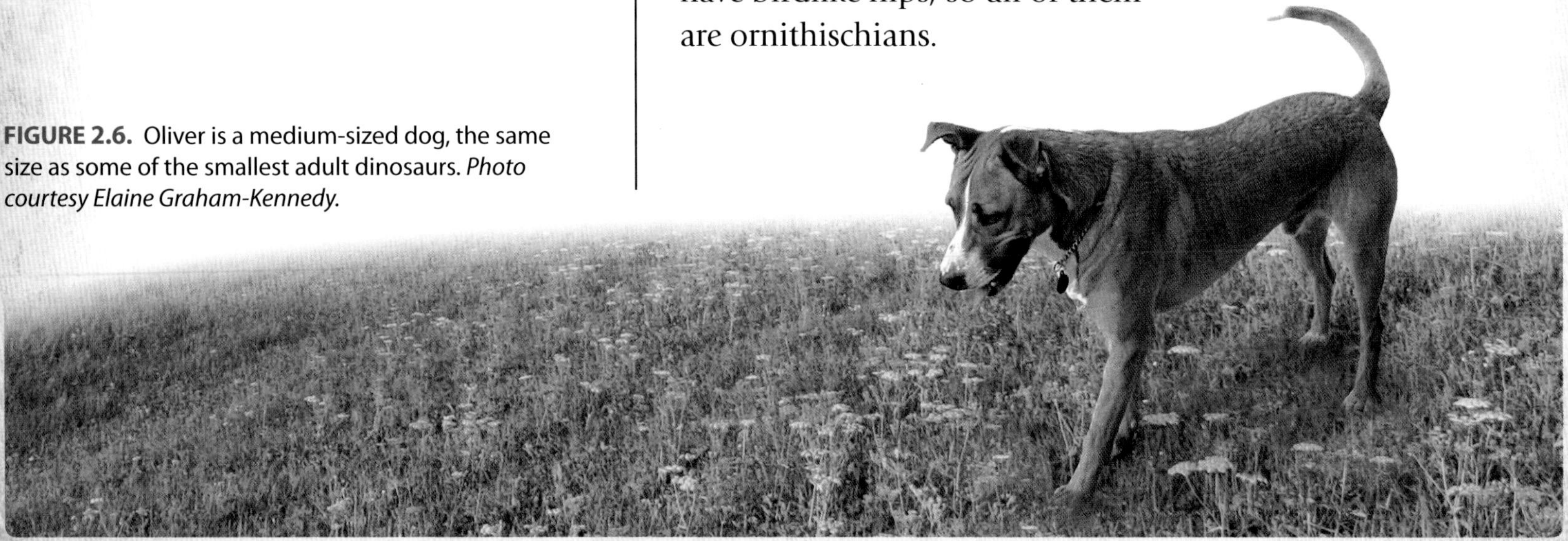

FIGURE 2.6. Oliver is a medium-sized dog, the same size as some of the smallest adult dinosaurs. *Photo courtesy Elaine Graham-Kennedy.*

Skeletons

Skeletons provide us with a general idea of the size and shape of the dinosaurs, but it is hard to know the exact shape and color of the animal. We have very little of the guts, muscles, or skin to look at, and that makes it hard to figure out exactly what they looked like.

Did you know that many dinosaurs were small? I didn't until I started studying them. I was really surprised at how tiny some of the dinosaurs were. A few were as small as a wild turkey. Others were the size of a large dog.

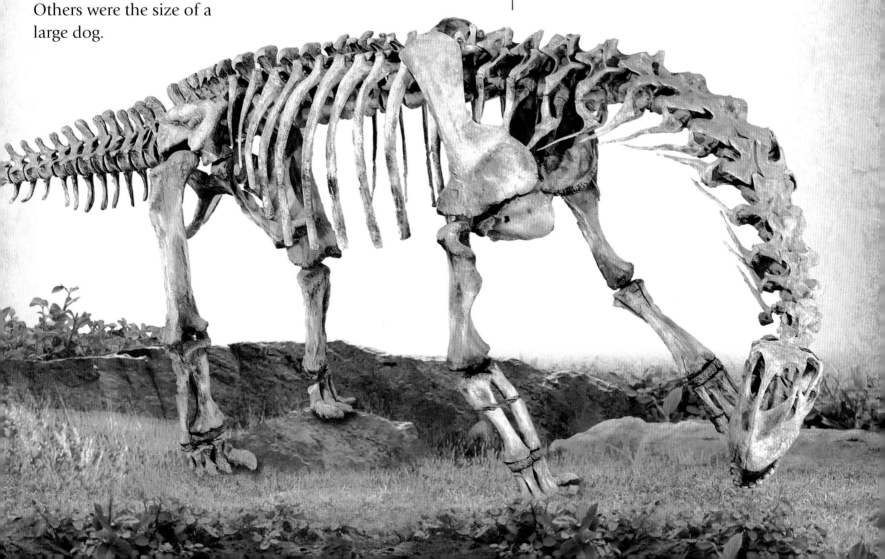

FIGURE 2.7. *Diplodocus* means "double beam." This dinosaur was about 90 feet (27.4 meters) long. *Photo courtesy Tyrrell Museum/Alberta Community Development.*

FIGURE 2.8. In addition to the large and small adult dinosaurs, scientists have found skeletons of baby dinosaurs. So what's not to love about this baby? *Photo courtesy Natural History Museum of Los Angeles County and Tyrrell Museum/Alberta Community Development.*

Many people think of the large dinosaurs when they hear someone talking about dinosaurs. Some Christians wonder about those very large animals. Were sauropods too big to go on Noah's ark? Were any dinosaurs on the ark?

The biggest dinosaurs were the sauropods, and they probably were too big for the ark. *Diplodocus*, like other sauropods, carried a lot of its body weight along the back, hips, and legs of its skeleton. Some of the bridges we have today were designed like the skeletons of these gigantic saurischian sauropods.

Sauropods present a problem for scientists. Remember, these huge animals ate plants. It must have taken a lot of plants to keep them alive. But there are very few plants in the rock layers where many fossils of the sauropods are found. Some scientists ask, "What did these dinosaurs eat?" Nobody knows.

Many Christians suggest an answer for this problem. They think that these sauropods weren't buried where they lived before the Flood. They think that either the animals migrated during the Flood or the Flood washed their dead bodies to the place where they were found. Scientists know that nearly all the mud and sand found with the dinosaur bones was moved there by water. They have also found dinosaur "highways," so they think some kinds of dinosaurs migrated. The movement of the bodies of the dinosaurs from where they lived fits both the scientific facts and the story of Noah.

While sauropods were probably too big for the ark, there were quite a number of small dinosaurs. The small saurischians were all carnivores (meat-eaters), but they could have been on the ark. The small ornithischians were herbivores (plant-eaters), so most Christians don't really have a problem with them being on the ark.

When you look at the list on page 22, you'll see just how tiny some dinosaurs were! OK, some of the "small" adults were more than six feet long (bigger than me). But some of the adults were only two feet long. The babies of those little dinosaurs must have been really small!

You might be wondering how we can tell the bones of small adult dinosaurs from the bones of young dinosaurs. The young dinosaurs have the epiphysis preserved near the ends of their long bones. (Epiphysis is like spongy bone or cartilage.) Kids like you have epiphysis in their bones too. It's where the bones grow. Epiphysis turns into hard bone when young animals become adults.

It is possible that any animals the size of a giraffe or elephant or smaller could have been on Noah's ark. That could have included the small dinosaurs. This doesn't prove that dinosaurs were on the ark or lived after the Flood. It also doesn't prove that the Genesis Flood killed the dinosaurs. Those beliefs are based on faith.

Some Christians think the dinosaurs all died because they were all very large. Do you think you could explain to them that many of the dinosaurs could have been on the ark? Would they believe you? If not, show them pictures of the real bones of the little adults!

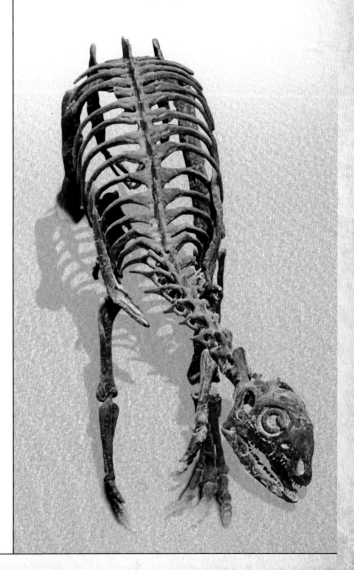

FIGURE 2.9. *Othnielia* was about the same size as Oliver, the medium sized dog. *Photo courtesy Timothy G. Standish and the North American Museum of Ancient Life, Thanksgiving Point, Utah.*

FIGURE 2.10. Elephant ride at the Santa Ana Zoo, California. *Photo courtesy Elaine Graham-Kennedy.*

CHECK THIS OUT!

Scientific Name	Common Name	Height or Length
Saurischians		
Coelurids		4–8 feet (1.2–2.4 m)
Coelophysids	Hollow forms	2–10 feet (0.6–3.0 m)
Compsognathids	Pretty jaws	2–3 feet (0.6–0.9 m)
Raptors	Thieves	6–10 feet (1.8–3.0 m)
Ornithischians		
Heterodontosaurids	Odd-teeth lizards	4 feet (1.2 m)
Hypsilophodontids	High-ridge teeth	3–8 feet (0.9–2.4 m)
Fabrosaurids		3 feet (0.9 m)
Pachycephalosaurids	Thick-head lizards	3–15 feet (0.9–4.6 m)
Homalocephalids	Identical heads	10–20 feet (3.0–6.0 m)
Scutellosaurids	Small-shield lizards	2–4 feet (0.6–1.2 m)
Protoceratopsids	First-horned faces	3–10 feet (0.9–3.0 m)
Psittacosaurids	Parrot lizard	6 feet (1.8 m)

The Bones of Tyrannosaurus rex

SOME CHRISTIANS don't like T-rex or the "raptors." They don't like any of the meat-eating theropods because both large and small theropods were powerful animals with very sharp teeth. They want to know if God created these vicious animals to live in the Garden of Eden. They want to know why a good God would create predators—animals that kill and eat other animals.

Today, predators play an important role in the animal kingdom. They limit the number of plant-eating animals by eating the sick and the weak. That helps keep the rest of these animals healthy.

Many Christians believe predation would not be needed in a perfect world. The Bible tells us a little about what the world was like before there were predators. It says that God gave every green plant to people and animals for food. God may have created "kinds" of theropods, but according to the Bible, He gave them green plants, not other animals, to eat.

So, how does the Bible explain the death of animals? It tells us that during Creation week God saw what He had made and said it was good. Some time later, a terrible thing happened. Adam and Eve decided to disobey God. They ate the fruit God had told them not to eat. Then everything changed. Adam and Eve became afraid of God. Plants with thorns and thistles began to grow. Adam and Eve had to leave the Garden. And they wore animal skins for clothing. The Bible talks about animals dying only after Adam and Eve sinned. This is a sad topic, but it helps us understand our world.

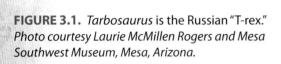

FIGURE 3.1. *Tarbosaurus* is the Russian "T-rex." *Photo courtesy Laurie McMillen Rogers and Mesa Southwest Museum, Mesa, Arizona.*

Some people think that death belongs in our world; it's just the way things are. But the Bible tells us why there is death in our world. It says that disobeying God causes death. When Adam and Eve disobeyed God, death became a part of the world. I don't believe God wanted anyone or any of His animals to die then or now.

FIGURE 3.2. *Tyrannosaurus rex. Photo courtesy Tyrrell Museum/Alberta Community Development.*

God wants us to live with Him forever. We choose to die when we choose to disobey God. But God sent Jesus to live and die for us so that we can live with Him forever.

Many people know this, but unfortunately, it hasn't helped them accept the beauty of T-rex. Lots of people say dinosaurs are ugly. Some people might think that T-rex was an ugly "killing machine," but I like this animal. It was so big and powerful—it was majestic! Just imagine what a T-rex looked like when God first created it!

FIGURE 3.3. Close-up view of the tip of a T-rex tooth. *Photo courtesy Southwest Adventist University Online Fossil Museum.*

The name *Tyrannosaurus rex* means "tyrant lizard king." It wasn't the biggest meat eater, but it is the best known. The famous T-rex named Sue was 39 feet (11.9 meters) long. It might have weighed as much as 7 tons (6.4 metric tons). That's 14,000 pounds (6,350 kilograms)! And its teeth were about 7 inches (17.8 centimeters) long.

Let's take a good look at T-rex. First, it is important to look carefully at the whole body of any dinosaur. Scientists do not have complete skeletons for most dinosaurs. Fortunately, scientists have found several nearly complete skeletons of T-rex, so we have a lot of information about them.

By using a microscope, we can see the structure of T-rexs' bones. The bones have little holes. You have holes like these, called vesicles, in your bones too. T-rexs also have growth lines in their bones similar to the ones we find in reptiles. No other animals have both the vesicles and the growth lines that dinosaurs have. This is one reason

Photo courtesy Tyrrell Museum/ Alberta Community Development.

some scientists think they aren't just big reptiles—that they're a separate group of animals. This difference also means that dinosaurs may have been created special by God. They're not reptiles, not birds, not mammals, not insects. They're not just like anything else.

But this also is an example of how different people can look at the facts about dinosaurs and decide that different things are true.

The strangest looking bones of T-rex are the arms. Many people think that they were too small to have helped T-rex do much. Some say the arms were too short to reach its mouth. Others think that if T-rex fell down, it couldn't use its arms to help it get up.

Scientists have studied the muscle attachment scars on skeletons, and they have gathered information about the nerves from the skeletons too. Based on this information, some researchers have done experiments testing the strength of muscles built like that. They think that T-rex could lift six hundred pounds with those tiny arms! They were strong enough for T-rex to carry its food and its young.

We will learn more about T-rex when we start looking at dinosaur skulls and teeth.

FIGURE 3.4. Structure of the bone of a typical dinosaur. *Photo courtesy Elaine Graham-Kennedy.*

FIGURE 3.5. Check out the tiny arms! *Photo courtesy Tyrrell Museum/Alberta Community Development.*

FIGURE 3.6. Many of the fossilized bones have rough areas called muscle attachment scars. The dinosaurs' muscles were attached to these rough areas. Some scientists study these scars to get an idea of the size and strength of the dinosaurs' muscles. *Photo courtesy Tyrrell Museum/Alberta Community Development.*

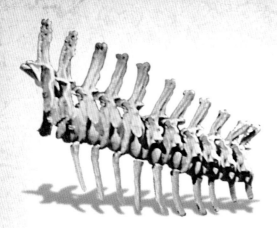

FIGURE 3.7. Scientists interpret the long chevrons (bones sticking out from the bottom of the vertebra) at the base of this *Diplodocus* tail to mean that this dinosaur was a male. *Photo courtesy Timothy G. Standish and the North American Museum of Ancient Life.*

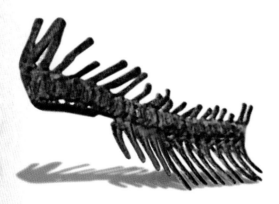

FIGURE 3.8. The shorter chevrons at the base of the *Triceratops* tail suggest that this was a female. The space created by the shorter chevrons may have allowed easier egg laying. *Photo courtesy Tyrrell Museum/Alberta Community Development.*

MORE BONE STUFF FROM OTHER DINOSAURS

There are some bones in the tails of dinosaurs that might be important. At the base of each tail are some bones that stick straight down. These bones are long on some dinosaurs. Scientists think those dinosaurs might have been boys. On other dinosaurs these same bones are short. The short bones would make egg laying easier, so some scientists think these dinosaurs were girls. It sounds good, but we can't prove that it's true. It's pretty interesting anyway, isn't it?

Here's another interesting feature: All the Dromaeosaurids have a big claw on their hind feet. The claw is curved and sticks up. Did they use the claw for fighting? For climbing? Did they use it for digging? Did they use it to kill their supper? No one knows for sure. They may have used it for any or all of the above.

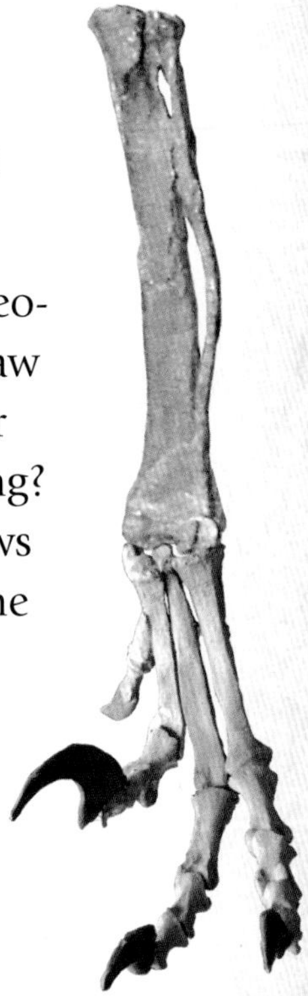

FIGURE 3.9. Dromaeosaurids ("running lizards"), including *Velociraptor* and *Deinonychus*, have a retracted toe and claw on their hind feet that they may have used for fighting. If this is true, these animals were very athletic. *Photo courtesy Timothy G. Standish and Geoscience Research Institute.*

Dinosaur Bones, Teeth, and Skulls

FIGURE 4.1B. Neck bones.

FIGURE 4.1A. These are photos of a *Velociraptor*, with close-ups of specific bones. *Photos courtesy Timothy G. Standish and the Geoscience Research Institute.*

YOU FIND MANY THINGS when you look in the dirt for dinosaurs. The most common things you find are bones. There are pieces of bones, whole bones, and even whole skeletons. Skulls and teeth are also buried in the earth. It is harder to find dinosaur tracks, and even harder to find the prints of dinosaurs' skin. Dinosaur eggs are very rare, but people have found some, and there must be more out there among the rocks. We'll talk about dinosaur bones, teeth, and skulls in this chapter and the tracks, skin prints, eggs, and nests in the next chapters. Remember, though: Digging for dinosaur bones in parks is against the law. You can look for dinosaur fossils on the ground. But if you find something, leave it there and report it!

Bones come in all shapes and sizes. Some bones are easy to identify. You know what bones look like, but can you tell a finger bone from a toe bone? You may need to look at a book to know what backbones look like, but could you pick out the leg bones and arm bones?

Can you tell a thighbone from a shinbone? There are a lot of bones to learn.

Let's look at a few bones so we'll have a better idea what certain types of them look like.

Can you guess the name of the dinosaur each bone came from? You would probably need a very good book to help you do that, so I put the dinosaur's name by the photo. Let's look at the skeleton first. The backbones don't all look alike, and the neck bones don't look like the backbones. Photo "B" is a close-up of the neck bones. Photo "C" shows a femur—the large thighbone. The other picture shows the phalanges—the finger and toe bones. Some dinosaur workers can look at just a few bones and tell you the name of the dinosaur. They *really* know their bones!

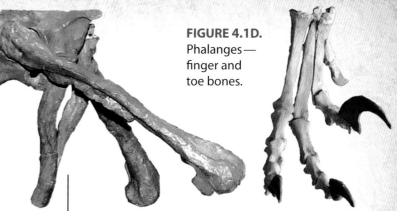

FIGURE 4.1D.
Phalanges—finger and toe bones.

FIGURE 4.1C.
Femur—large thighbone.

LOOK FOR TEETH

Scientists study teeth to identify some dinosaurs and to figure out what dinosaurs ate. T-rex had teeth about seven inches long. Sometimes their teeth broke off while they were eating. The teeth that were lost are called "shed teeth." The edges had sharp ridges, like the knives people use to cut meat. Scientists have found broken T-rex teeth in bones of other animals. So they think T-rex and other theropods ate meat. I think the facts support this idea pretty well.

Allosaurus ("strange lizard") is another theropod that loses its teeth when it eats. Look at the photo of its upper jaw (fig. 4-3).

Plant-eating dinosaurs had a very different jaw structure from that of the theropods. The ceratopsians (horned dinosaurs) had "beaks" and "dental batteries"—rows of teeth. They had lots of teeth,

FIGURE 4.2. These vertebrae (backbones) are from a fairly large dinosaur. Notice the lines of the bones and how similar the bone color is to the color of the dirt. That makes it hard to see the bones. You have to look carefully for them! *Photo courtesy Dinosaur National Monument, Jensen, Utah.*

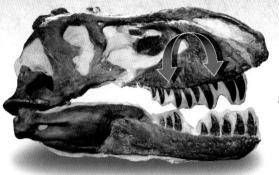

FIGURE 4.3. Arrows point to new teeth in this upper jaw of an allosaur. *Photo courtesy Tyrrell Museum/Alberta Community Development.*

but no more than six hundred of them. The upper and lower teeth were lined up in such a way that they used only one row of teeth as they ate. Their teeth are not the typical grinding teeth of plant-eating animals. Their diet may have consisted of tough, fibrous plants that their teeth chopped. As usual, we don't know for sure.

Another dinosaur with dental batteries was the hadrosaur. However, the side teeth of the hadrosaurs were angled to form chewing teeth that were self-sharpening as they ate. These dino–saurs had dental batteries with as many as six hundred to a thousand teeth. As new teeth grew, they replaced the worn, older teeth. Some hadrosaurs may have used their front teeth to nip off small tree branches and other woody tissue of conifers (evergreens, such as pine trees).

FIGURE 4.4. *Zuniceratops* had a jaw structure similar to other ceratopsians. *Photo by Laurie McMillen Rogers, courtesy Mesa Southwest Museum, Arizona.*

FIGURE 4.5. The hadrosaur (duck-billed) dinosaurs had teeth positioned for self-sharpening. *Photo courtesy Southwest Adventist University Online Fossil Museum.*

Scientists are interested in what each kind of dinosaur ate. In very rare cases, they've found stuff they believe was in a dinosaur's stomach when the dinosaur died. And in Montana, they found a hard rock in soft mud rock layers. The rock had many bits of wood in it, and holes like those made by dung beetles. Scientists think it is dinosaur dung because people have found many duck-billed dinosaurs in this area. (Dung is poop.) If it is dung, they can't know for sure who dropped it, but it might have been those hadrosaurs.

Now that you have looked at some of the teeth, what do you think the dinosaurs were eating?

FIGURE 4.6. This rock might be real dinosaur dung. *Photo courtesy Montana Nature Conservancy.*

Study the Skulls

Since there are no dinosaurs alive today, it's hard to figure out how they acted. But scientists want to know, so they use every method they can think of to try to understand them. Remember, we want to learn as much as we can about these animals too because we want to understand their place in God's world.

FIGURE 4.7. The T-rex brain had enlarged optic (sight) and olfactory (smell) lobes, so scientists have had some good discussions about the feeding habits of T-rex! *Photo courtesy Tyrrell Museum/Alberta Community Development.*

Some scientists try to guess how dinosaurs lived by studying their brains. They want to know how smart dinosaurs were. They fill dinosaur skulls with gooey plastic and then remove it when it gets hard. Then they can tell the shape of the brain that fit inside the skull. These scientists compare the casts of the dinosaurs' brains with the casts of brains of animals that are alive today. Here are some of the brain features that scientists have seen in modern animals:

FIGURE 4.8. *Stegosaurus* had a brain the size of a walnut. *Photo courtesy Tyrrell Museum/ Alberta Community Development.*

- In predators (animals that kill other animals for food), the part of the brain that controls seeing is larger than in most other animals.

- In scavengers (animals that eat other animals they find that are already dead), the part of the brain that controls the sense of smell is larger than in most other animals.

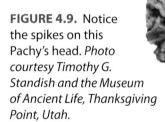

FIGURE 4.9. Notice the spikes on this Pachy's head. *Photo courtesy Timothy G. Standish and the Museum of Ancient Life, Thanksgiving Point, Utah.*

The brains of the plant-eating dinosaurs were very small compared to the size of their bodies. That might mean they weren't very smart. However, scientists have discovered that comparing the size of the brain to the body may not tell us how smart modern grazing animals are. It is only an estimate. So, a dinosaur's brain-to-body size may not tell us its real brainpower either.

FIGURE 4.10.
The large frill of the *Chasmosaurus* may have been very colorful. *Photo courtesy Tyrrell Museum/Alberta Community Development.*

Skulls are fascinating because they come in all shapes and sizes. The skulls of some of the armored dinosaurs have some really unusual features.

The name *Pachycephalosaurus* means "thick-headed lizard." It wasn't really a lizard, of course, because it was a dinosaur. It was approximately 15 feet (4.6 meters) long and had a very thick skull—about 10 inches (25.4 centimeters) thick. Books and museums often show Pachys charging each other with their heads down. But they probably didn't behave that way. Their skull bones were thick, but they weren't solid and hard. Most of the Pachys have a line of knobs around the skull that may have been the bottom part of their spikes.

Ceratopsians (the horned dinosaurs) have a variety of skull shapes with elaborate frills. (Frills are large extensions of bone from the back of the skull over the back of the neck.) Some scientists think the frills helped the ceratopsians regulate their body temperature. Other scientists think the ceratopsians used their frills to attract mates or perhaps to threaten or intimidate other dinosaurs. Or they may have protected the neck from predators. Nobody knows for sure.

What do you think about the frill? Colorful frills would have been really beautiful!

We can learn more from dinosaur skulls. For example, different kinds of dinosaurs have their eyes at different places on their heads. This might mean some dinosaurs could see better than other dinosaurs. Today, predators (meat-eaters) have their eyes on the front of their faces. They can see things that are standing still. Prey (plant-eaters, which predators eat) have their eyes on the sides of their heads. They can detect movement well. Look carefully at the eye positions of the *Velociraptor* and the *Triceratops*. You can tell by where the eyes are placed that *Velociraptor* (the predator) could see to the front and the sides, but the *Triceratops* (the prey) could see only to the sides.

VELOCIRAPTOR

FIGURE 4.11. Notice how big the eye sockets of the *Velociraptor* are as compared to the eye sockets of the *Triceratops*. *Photo of the* Triceratops *courtesy Tyrrell Museum/Alberta Community Development. Photo of the* Velociraptor *Timothy G. Standish and the Geoscience Research Institute.*

TRICERATOPS

CONNECT THE BONES

Here's a pile of dinosaur bones. See if you can match the body bones (marked with letters) with the skulls they belong to (marked with numbers). The answers are upside down below.

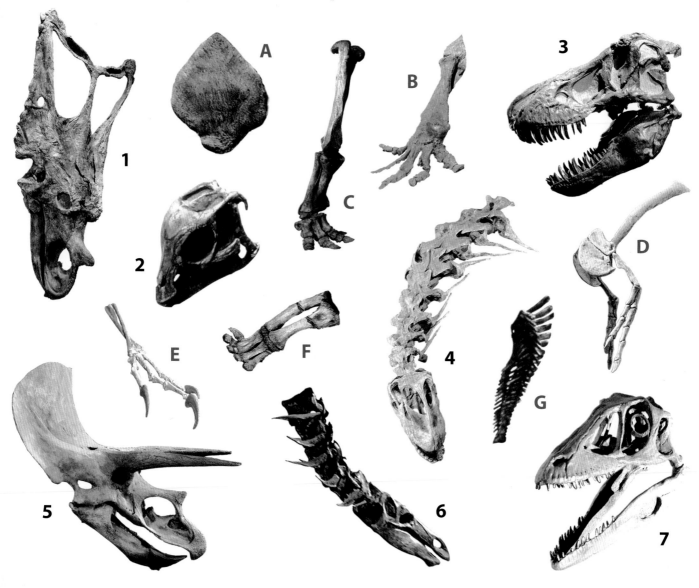

Dinosaur Tracks

FIGURE 5.1. From each footprint impression (depending on how good it is), scientists may be able to learn the shape of the foot and the shape of the ball of the foot (foot pad), the number of toes and the length and width of each, the shape of the claws, the skin texture of the foot, and the direction of travel. *Photo from Bureau of Land Management, Utah, courtesy Elaine Graham-Kennedy.*

YEARS AGO, some people were taught that dinosaurs never really lived. They thought the dinosaur bones were fakes. Today, we know the dinosaurs really were alive because we find their tracks.

Tracks are footprints in mud or sand that animals make as they walk, run, or hop. Dead animals don't make tracks. So, when we find dinosaur tracks, we can be pretty sure that dinosaurs really lived sometime in the past! The question is, how did the dinosaurs get here? What do you think?

Many Christians believe God created dinosaurs. Other Christians think Satan made the dinosaur bones to fool us. As you will soon see, Satan would have had to make a lot of different kinds of dinosaur bones, skin marks, tracks, and eggs all over the world. I don't think he did. I think he tries to convince people that God is not their Creator.

Still other Christians think some animals changed into dinosaurs over a very long time. However, we have learned from nature and from experiments that animals can change only a little. There are limits to change in all animals. Special breeding programs have changed the way dogs look, but large or small, long-nosed or short-nosed, they are still dogs. They never change into some other kind of animal.

After looking at the facts from science, history, and the Bible, I think God created the dinosaurs. I also think that the Bible's story about the history of our earth is true.

Animal tracks are found in stone all around the world. Animals make them when they walk or run across mud that later hardens into rock. But we don't always know what animal made the tracks. We hardly ever find animals that have dropped dead in their tracks. Some of the smaller tracks that some people think dinosaurs made may not be dinosaur tracks at all. However, scientists are more confident regarding the larger tracks.

It's hard to figure out which dinosaur made which tracks. Even though we know what the foot bones of the dinosaurs looked like, we don't know what the feet looked like when muscles and skin covered those bones. So, scientists can only tell us which dinosaur they *think* made a particular track.

There are many animal tracks, including tracks of birds, found in rock layers with the dinosaur tracks. But there are no human tracks with dinosaur tracks. Some people think there are, but some very good Christians who are scientists studied what people thought were human tracks and discovered that they weren't real tracks. Since we haven't found human tracks and dinosaur tracks together, most scientists think humans didn't live at the same time dinosaurs did.

Some Christians think that dinosaurs lived with people after the Flood. They think that dinosaurs were what people called dragons long, long ago. But there are no dinosaur bones or tracks in the rocks where human bones or tracks are found. This means that we can't prove that humans and dinosaurs lived together at the same time, either before the Flood or after it.

Some people say that the Christians who believe that dinosaurs and people lived at the same time are ignoring the scientific facts.

FIGURE 5.2. Bird tracks. *Photo courtesy Timothy G. Standish.*

FIGURE 5.3. With a little imagination, the outlined area looks like the imprint of a human foot, but there is no human track here. The real track is the larger area darkned with water. It's a sauropod track! *Photo courtesy Glen Rose State Park, Texas.*

However, the scientific facts can't *prove* these Christians are wrong. So far, we haven't found the tracks of dinosaurs with the footprints of people. And we haven't found the bones of a person with the bones of a dinosaur. (It would be *great* if we found the head of a person in the jaws of a T-rex. OK, it wouldn't be very good for that person, but it would be great for us.) However, while we can't find these facts, this proof, that doesn't mean that something didn't happen. When we can't find it, we can't prove it one way or the other.

Also, facts don't *prove* anyone is wrong because facts don't tell us what to believe. Facts help people *think* about what they believe. People choose what to believe by thinking about the facts.

Some people make choices based on only one kind of facts. Some scientists think only about the facts from nature. Some Christians think only about the facts from the Bible. When people think only about one kind of facts, they tend to make too much of their ideas. This is true whether they are basing their ideas on the facts from science, the Bible or history, or on any other set of facts from a single source.

Many Christians believe that the Bible tells us important facts about life on earth, and I agree. But what do we do if the facts from nature and the facts from the Bible seem to say two different things? This is a tough question to answer. Sometimes we understand the Bible better when we have more facts from nature. I think we need to study all the facts, not just the facts from nature, the Bible, or history. What do you believe?

Based on the Bible's story of our earth and the track information, many Christians think that humans and dinosaurs lived at the same time but not in the same places. Did dinosaurs and humans live together? What do you think? Perhaps scientists will find real human and dinosaur tracks together in the same place one day.

WATCH FOR TRACKS

Scientists study each track as they look for really good tracks. Good tracks show the shape of the foot and may even show some things about the skin on the foot. Scientists can locate the ball of the foot, the number of toes, the length and width of each foot, and the claw marks. They find the direction the dinosaur was going by using a compass.

FIGURE 5.4. Theropod tracks. *Photo courtesy Glen Rose State Park, Texas.*

Sometimes scientists find three or more tracks in a line. A line of tracks gives us even more information about the dinosaur's movement:

- Two or four track marks can tell us the size of the steps the dinosaur took as it walked.

- Two or four tracks can tell us how the animal stood.

- Short steps mixed with long steps in one line may mean the animal was limping.

- The foot size and stride (the size of the steps) and some math can tell us how fast the dinosaur probably moved. (Unfortunately, we can't know for certain the dinosaur's speed, but we can assume that if two dinosaurs had feet and strides that are the same size, they probably moved at the same speed.)

FIGURE 5.5. How many lines of tracks can you find?

FIGURE 5.6.
This surface
is heavily
worn, and
these holes
may not
be dinosaur
tracks.
Research
requires
very careful
examination
of the data.
*Photo was
taken near
Isona, Spain.
Photo courtesy
Elaine Graham-
Kennedy.*

If you pretend that two dinosaurs have the same size feet but one dinosaur has long legs and the other dinosaur has short legs, then the length of the steps they make will be different even though they're both just walking. If you use math without knowing the length of the legs, the numbers will tell you the taller dinosaur was running. This is why numbers are not always facts.

Scientists make maps of tracks. They use these maps to suggest what the dinosaurs might have been doing. These maps tell us where the dinosaurs were moving.

Based on the arrangement and size of the tracks, some dinosaurs may have moved in herds. The tracks appear organized, with small tracks (the young?) in the center and the larger tracks (adults?) along the outside. However, it is important to remember that this may not reflect normal behavior. Some Christians think the tracks might tell us something about the unusual conditions that occurred during the Genesis Flood.

Today most tracks get washed away by water or blown away by wind. Scientists think the sun baked some dinosaur tracks, but they think most tracks were made under water. They think some of the tracks were made at the edge of a lake and others were made on a beach. They think mud slowly filled the tracks and saved them. But tracks at the edges of lakes and oceans wash away quickly. It is more likely that the good tracks were made as dinosaurs walked through shallow standing water. The weight of the large dinosaurs would have compressed the sand and mud, leaving deep prints. As they walked, they would have stirred fine mud and clay into the water. When the clay settled out of the water, it could have formed a natural "glue" that protected the surface of the tracks. A little later, moving water or wind might have dropped more sand on top of the tracks without disturbing them.

Some prints may not be dinosaur tracks at all! Stingrays make holes or pits in mud on the bottom of the ocean as they feed or rest. Some of the holes found in rock may have been formed by stingrays instead of being footprints of big dinosaurs. When rain and wind have worn away the surface of the ground, finding out what the pits are becomes very hard.

Some scientists think that stingrays might have made the holes in figure 5.6. Others think they are dinosaur tracks. As you can see, people have to think very carefully when they try to figure out what made holes like these.

FIGURE 5.7. Modern stingray pit. *Photo courtesy Nick Hope (bubblevision.com).*

South Korea

United States

United States

United States

Israel

Israel

Skin Marks, Eggs, and Nests

FIGURE 6.1. This is a skin impression of a *Corytho-saurus. Photo courtesy Natural History Museum of Los Angeles County.*

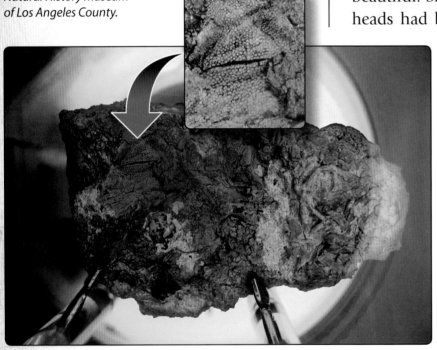

FIGURE 6.2. Embryo skin and bones have been reported. This material is from research conducted in Patagonia, Argentina. *Photo courtesy Natural History Museum of Los Angeles County.*

ANYONE INTERESTED in dinosaurs would love to know what they really looked like. Workers look under dinosaur bones for marks made in the dirt by the dinosaur's skin. It is rare to find skin marks. It is even harder to find mummified skin! Remember, skin is soft tissue and needs just the right conditions to keep it from decaying.

Some of the skin marks scientists have found show that the belly of a dinosaur was smoother than the back. Some of the marks show patterns that suggest some dinosaurs may have been very beautiful. Skin marks under a sauropod skull tell us that their heads had bumps and lumps and perhaps even some sharp points! In Canada, people have found ceratopsian skin impressions that have five-sided and six-sided patterns. Scientists have found baby skin marks in eggs too.

FIND EGGS AND EGGSHELL PIECES

When we find eggs, we know that the animals they belong to are alive and having babies. It doesn't matter whether the eggs are from birds or turtles or butterflies, we get excited about the eggs because we know that there are babies growing inside. They are a part of the miracle of life that God has given to us.

How do you know when you find a dinosaur egg? It's not always easy to tell because different kinds of dinosaurs laid different kinds of eggs, and some of the eggs are small enough to be bird or reptile eggs. A few of the eggs that have been found had baby dinosaurs inside, but most do not. Some fossil eggs are very large (bigger than ostrich eggs!). They are probably too large to be bird eggs. Sometimes dinosaur bones are found with the eggs. One time, workers found dinosaur bones with eggshells, but the eggshells and bones were not from the same dinosaurs.

Some workers think if they find one egg, they've found a nest. Others think real nests will have many eggs. It takes more than eggs to make a nest. Scientists must look carefully at the rocks around the eggs to be sure there is evidence that a dinosaur made a nest there.

Many times the mud and sand that became rock show that a current of water put the eggs in place. Lots of people think eggs break too easily to survive being moved by water. However, some might have floated into place, and, since eggs are very rounded, others might have rolled there. The condition of the sand and mud around dinosaur eggs shows that water moved most of the eggs.

.24 inches (6 mm)

FIGURE 6.3. Eggshells have three layers, and the structure of the dinosaur eggs is sometimes very well preserved. *Photo courtesy Lee Spencer.*

FIGURE 6.4. Eggs and eggshells vary in size, shape, and thickness. This egg from France has a very thin shell. *Photo from Provence, France, courtesy Elaine Graham-Kennedy.*

FIGURE 6.6. This egg in South Korea is an elongated, thin-shelled variety. *Photo from Korean Nature Conservancy, courtesy Elaine Graham-Kennedy.*

FIGURE 6.5. These eggshell fragments from Argentina are from large, thick-shelled eggs. *Photo from Rio Negro Province, Argentina, courtesy Elaine Graham-Kennedy.*

FIGURE 6.7. Summertime temperatures in Patagonia can exceed one hundred degrees Fahrenheit. Fortunately, it is a dry heat, and that makes the temperatures more bearable. (Yes, that's me having a bad hair day!) *Photo courtesy Lee Spencer.*

FIGURE 6.8. Here is an eggshell fragment before it was removed from the mudstone. *Photo courtesy Lee Spencer.*

Some places in Montana, Mongolia, and France seem to have eggs in three different levels of the rock. Eggs in South Korea have also been found on three levels. Some eggs in Argentina are found on at least three levels. It appears that wind or water moved those eggs.

More than one level of eggs may mean that dinosaurs made nests in the same place year after year, as many birds do today. Of course, that wouldn't be true if water or wind moved the eggs to the places where they were buried in the sand and mud and became rock.

If dinosaurs laid these eggs in different years, then it would mean the eggs couldn't have been laid during the one year of the Genesis Flood. However, the rock near the eggs must be studied carefully because in many places water has moved the eggs from the nesting grounds and left them where they've been found.

It is also possible that as nests were made and eggs were being laid, sands and muds were being washed in and rapidly covering the eggs. If conditions were right, mineral-rich waters could have soaked the eggs, preserving them and the embryos. If this is true, then different dinosaurs could have deposited the eggs fairly rapidly during the Genesis Flood.

MY DINOSAUR EGG RESEARCH

Let me tell you a little bit about my own research. I worked in Patagonia, Argentina, during several summers. (Summers there are in January and February, and they are very hot!) Scraggly looking bushes, small cacti, and gorgeous cliffs of sandstone and mudstone fill the landscape. One bush there grows quite large and has a very oily sap. A local rancher told us that if we got into trouble day or night, we should set this kind of bush on fire. At night, the fire is visible for a few miles, and in the daytime, the black smoke can be seen from an even greater distance!

We usually woke up just before sunrise for breakfast. Then we packed up and hiked for about an hour to the work site. We could not dig for the dinosaur eggs and eggshell fragments with shovels or picks. Instead, we used the small tools that dentists use so we wouldn't miss anything. It took more than two weeks for two of us to measure the position of more than two hundred eggshell fragments in a two-square-meter area (about two square yards).

We excavated clusters of eggs from cross-bedded sandstone. Cross-beds of sandstone form when wind or water transports sand. Even though the eggs seem to be clustered together, they are actually scattered throughout the sand. This suggests that the sand and eggs were rolled along together as they were moved from some other area to this site.

FIGURE 6.9. Blue arrows mark eggs; red arrow marks cross-beds. *Photo from author's field site courtesy Roberto Biaggi.*

FIGURE 6.10. Patagonian landscape. *Photo courtesy Roberto Biaggi.*

FIGURE 6.11. This sauropod egg was reconstructed by our Argentine collaborator, Professor Carlos Steger, who was invaluable to the work in Patagonia for many years as liaison, interpreter, guide, and friend. *Photo courtesy Carlos Steger.*

FIGURE 6.12. Eggshell fragments littered the ground at the "Nest-in-Camp" in Montana. *Photo from author's field site at Nature Conservancy west of Choteau, Montana. Photo courtesy Elaine Graham-Kennedy.*

I also worked at an egg site near Choteau, Montana. We worked a hilltop near the camp of other researchers. Thin, black shell fragments littered the ground. We planned to do a study similar to the one we had done in Patagonia.

Unfortunately, halfway through our excavation of the dig site, we came across two broken eggs. Normally, finding an egg is exciting. However, this time, the person in charge of the digging decided that we should stop our work. But from the work we had done, we were able to determine that this wasn't a nest site but a place to which eggs were carried by water and dropped in a "crevasse splay."

Crevasse splays form when water breaks across the natural edge of a riverbank and spills onto flat ground beside the river. The flooding water digs a bowl-shaped hole on the flat surface of this floodplain and deposits sand and mud. Then water is trapped in the holes, and mud from the river settles out of the water and covers the muddy sands.

FIGURE 6.13. After working the site for a week and a half, field assistant Jeff Graham found this broken egg. Minutes later, I found a second one nearby. *Photo courtesy Elaine Graham-Kennedy.*

In our crevasse splay, the eggs rolled in with the muddy water and settled in the sandy hole. Some of the eggs broke completely apart, leaving scattered eggshell fragments within the mud. Other eggs were only partially broken, and some were intact. (A group of people who worked in another part of the splay had already removed the intact eggs.) What we had thought might be a real nest turned out to be transported material.

Where to Find a Dinosaur

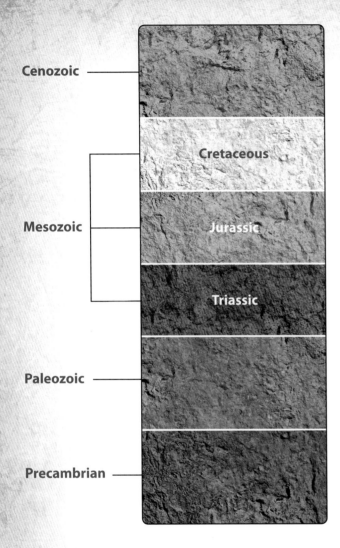

Cenozoic

Cretaceous

Mesozoic — Jurassic

Triassic

Paleozoic

Precambrian

FIGURE 7.1. Simplified geologic chart showing the names for the major layers of rocks.

Stegosaurus pictured on page 51. *Photo courtesy Tyrrell Museum/Alberta Community Development.*

NOW YOU KNOW a little about dinosaur fossils— what they look like. But if you wanted to find dinosaur fossils, where would you go?

Some scientists study more than the bones. They study the rock where they find the bones because they want to know how the dinosaurs died and were buried. This research has been really important and has provided a lot of good information.

Here is the bad news: Dinosaur fossils are in rock layers that may not be in your backyard. They are found in the Mesozoic ("middle life") rocks. These rocks are divided into three units. The chart shows that the lowest rocks in the group are the Triassic rocks. These rocks are well known for their red color. Dinosaur bones are found in the upper layers of the Triassic rocks worldwide. Scientists refer to these rock deposits as the first appearance of the dinosaurs in the rock record. Many Christians would say that the dinosaurs in the Triassic rocks were probably the first dinosaurs to die during the Genesis Flood.

The last of the dinosaur fossils are found in the Cretaceous rocks. These rocks contain a lot of chalk layers, such as the white cliffs of Dover in England. Scientists refer to the uppermost Cretaceous layers as the rocks containing the last appearance of the dinosaurs. Many Christians, of course, believe these rocks contain the last of the dinosaurs killed by the Flood.

Most dinosaur bones lie in layers of sand and mud that have become rock. Storms and floods laid this stuff across large areas. Dinosaurs are found in flood layers in Canada. They are found in hard mud rocks in the United States. People dig dinosaurs from mud rocks in South America and from boulder beds and mud rocks in Southeast Asia. Some scientists discovered dinosaurs in sandstones and mud rocks in China. Some are found in sandstones and mud rocks in Europe.

Workers find almost all dinosaur bones in mud rocks and sandstones deposited by water. However, most scientists believe that little floods that happened in rivers, oceans, and lakes made these rocks. They don't believe in the kind of flood the Bible tells us about—one that covered the whole world.

As you can see in the following pages, dinosaurs are found all over the world!

More than one thousand dinosaur tracks have been reported worldwide. And dinosaur eggs have been found around the world too. We don't often find the tracks and eggs with the bones of the animals that produced them. So we can't be sure that all of these tracks and eggs came from dinosaurs. As you can see, the track map and egg map are similar to the dinosaur bone maps.

FIGURE 7.2. The white cliffs of Dover, England, are chalks made of the skeletons of coccoliths. Coccoliths are one-celled animals that live in the ocean. *Photo courtesy Elaine Graham-Kennedy.*

Photo courtesy Dreamstime.com

WORLDWIDE DISTRIBUTION OF THEROPOD DINOSAURS

 Triassic Theropods

 Jurassic Theropods

 Cretaceous Theropods

WORLDWIDE DISTRIBUTION OF SAUROPOD DINOSAURS

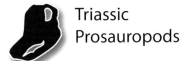 Triassic Prosauropods

 Jurassic Sauropods

 Cretaceous Sauropods

WORLDWIDE DISTRIBUTION OF ORNITHISCHIAN DINOSAURS

 Triassic Ornithischian

 Jurassic Ornithischian

 Cretaceous Ornithischian

WORLDWIDE DISTRIBUTION OF DINOSAUR TRACKS

 Dinosaur Tracks

WORLDWIDE DISTRIBUTION OF DINOSAUR EGGS

 Dinosaur Eggs

CHRISTIANS STUDY THE ROCKS

Among the scientists who are Christians, some aren't surprised that dinosaur bones are in rocks made by floods. They believe those sandstones and mud rocks came from the Genesis Flood.

These scientists believe the boulders, sands, muds, and water moved a lot during the Flood. This movement could make many layers of rock filled with dead plants and animals. Rain wasn't the only thing that happened during the year of the Flood. Lots of other things seem to have happened then too. The Bible tells us a little about what happened to the earth during that time. Studying the rocks and fossils of the earth tells us other things that happened.

No one knows for certain how the dinosaur bones got where we find them today. Everyone looks at the same rocks and the same bones, but some people think about other facts too. Christians read the Bible and think about the facts they find there. After people have looked at a lot of facts, they choose what they will believe. Do you know what you believe?

The scientists who believe the Bible do not all agree about what happened or how it happened. However, they know that scientific ideas are constantly changing, and they know that God's Word doesn't change. They believe that a lot of the evidence in the rocks supports what the Bible teaches about earth history. When they have to choose between the Bible's teachings and the theories of science, they choose to believe the Bible. They don't let theories from science tell them what to believe about the Bible.

Photo courtesy Dreamstime.com

These scientists who are Christian are very careful thinkers. They don't believe everything other people tell them the Bible says about scientific facts. They study both the Bible and science for themselves because sometimes people who talk about the Bible don't really understand it. These scientists who are Christian believe we find the truth where the Bible and scientific facts agree.

Photo courtesy
Dreamstime.com

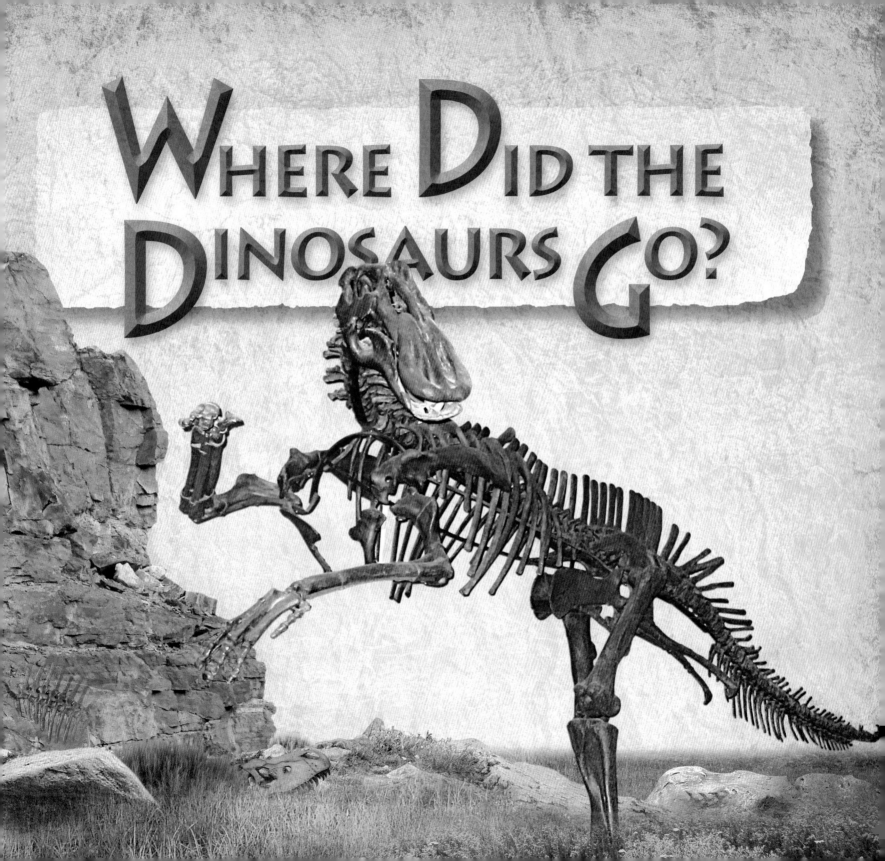

FIGURE 8.1. Although dromaeosaurids were small, lizard-hipped carnivores, some scientists think these dinosaurs were the ancestors of birds. This *Velociraptor* is one kind of dromaeosaur. *Photo courtesy Timothy G. Standish and the Geoscience Research Institute.*

WHAT HAPPENED to the dinosaurs? Why aren't any still living today? People have thought up many answers to these questions. Some people believe all the dinosaurs died over a long period of time. Some think they all died suddenly. Others think some of the dinosaurs evolved into birds.

Did they starve to death because of a change in weather over millions of years? Did a weather change cause the plants to die too? Did big volcanoes kill them quickly? Did meteorites hit the earth and kill them? Did the Genesis Flood destroy the dinosaurs?

People have asked these important questions about the end of dinosaurs. We may find some answers by studying the facts in nature, and we may find other answers in the Bible. Everyone studies the facts in nature. However, many Christians believe God created the dinosaurs a few thousand years ago. They think dinosaurs are just like all the other beautiful animals God made. They also believe that the worldwide Flood destroyed the dinosaurs along with many other animals. There are good facts to support this idea, but we cannot prove it.

Some people think that if no one can prove that the Flood happened and killed the dinosaurs, it must not have happened. But they can't prove that dinosaurs slowly turned into birds or that they died when a meteorite hit the earth either. You've been reading about dinosaurs. Have you read in Genesis about the Flood? What do you think happened to the dinosaurs?

Some scientists think dinosaurs are a link to birds. Some think a bird similar to *Archaeopteryx* was a link. The idea that birds came from dinosaurs is very popular. However, not all of the scientists who study dinosaurs and birds believe this. They think there are good reasons to keep birds in their own group. The best way to test any idea is to study the facts.

FACTS ABOUT BONES AND HIPS

The Triassic dinosaur *Coelophysis* had hollow bones. Birds also have hollow bones. That's one reason some scientists think there might be a link between the two. They see another link, too. The Cretaceous dromaeosaurs were small dinosaurs. Their hipbones were positioned toward the back of their bodies. Remember, the dromaeosaurs were saurischian dinosaurs. Because of the shape of the dromaeosaur hips, some scientists believe that the hipbones of the dinosaurs were becoming more like birds' hipbones.

Scientists have studied the hollow bones from one group of dinosaurs, hipbones from another group, and other facts too. Because of these facts, some of them believe that the birds descended from dinosaurs. However, *many* changes would have to happen for dinosaurs to turn into birds. Changes in the bones aren't enough. There are other facts we need to think about.

Coelophysis

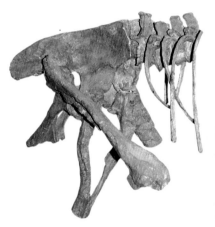

Dromaeosaur

Modern Bird

FIGURE 8.2. Look at the difference between the hip structure of the *Coelophysis*, the dromaeosaur, and a modern bird. *Photos courtesy Natural History Musuem of Los Angeles County, Geoscience Research Institute, and Timothy G. Standish, respectively.*

FIGURE 8.3.
Confuciusornis has been found in the Jurassic rocks of China.
Photo courtesy Timothy G. Standish.

FIGURE 8.4.
Archaeopteryx was a very unusual animal. Scientists think that the link to birds was probably an animal much like *Archaeopteryx*. Photo courtesy Musuem für Naturkunde, Berlin.

FACTS FROM THE ROCK LAYERS

Confuciusornis was a true bird. It was found buried in rock layers that had formed *before* the rock layers with the dromaeosaur bones were formed. So, according to many scientists, the first birds lived, died, and were buried in the rocks before the dromaeosaurs lived. This makes it unlikely that dromaeosaurs could be the ancestors of birds.

FACTS FROM ARCHAEOPTERYX

Scientists have found only a few fossils of *Archaeopteryx*. All of the bones come from rock in Germany. Scientists have studied these bones. Some of the *Archaeopteryx*'s bones are like reptile bones. Some are like bird bones.

Archaeopteryx also had feathers. Years ago, some scientists thought the impressions of the feathers in the rock were fakes. Other scientists studied the feather imprints and decided they were real. A single feather was found in these rocks, but no one can prove the feather came from *Archaeopteryx*. The feather looks like a modern bird feather.

Some of the bones in the *Archaeopteryx* skeletons are found only in this animal. These bones mean that it is not the link between dinosaurs and birds. Most scientists now think the link was some other animal that was similar to *Archaeopteryx*.

FACTS ABOUT BREATHING

When you breathe, air flows into your nose and across "shelves" within your nose. These "shelves" warm the air before it gets to your lungs. Dinosaur nostrils don't have these "shelves," but birds do.

When you want to take a big breath, a big muscle below your lungs moves to pull air into your lungs. Birds don't have this muscle. Some people think that dinosaurs had a muscle like this in their bodies, but others think they didn't. To know for sure, we need a lot of soft-tissue fossils from dinosaurs. However, we don't have many of that kind of fossil. Some scientists see what they think could be other evidence for these changes. They believe the changes show that birds came from the saurischian dinosaurs.

Scientists have found a lot of facts about dinosaurs. But what do these facts mean? Scientists explain the facts in many ways. No one knows all the answers. Remember, we don't know what the guts of all the dinosaurs looked like. Maybe some day we will know more.

Many Christians believe that dinosaurs and birds are different kinds of animals. They believe this because of what the Bible says about Creation. You've looked at the bones of birds, and you've looked at a lot of dinosaur bones. Did birds evolve from dinosaurs, or are they two different kinds of animals? Have you read what the Bible says about the creation of animals?

You need to study the facts to decide what you think. You need to know why you think something is true.

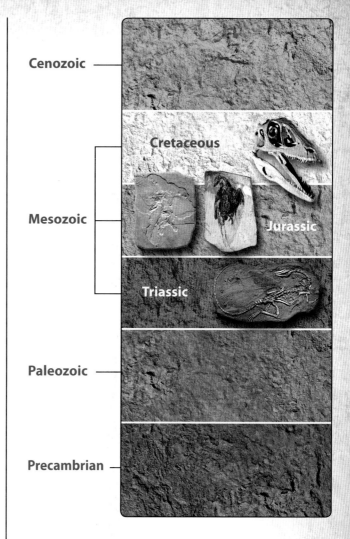

FIGURE 8.5. Here is the order in which the dinosaurs and birds are buried in the rock (from the top down) Remember: The Cretaceous animals were buried on top of (after) the Jurassic animals were buried. The Jurassic animals were buried on top of the Triassic animals.

WHERE DO YOU LIVE?

DO YOU LIVE NEAR AN
AREA WHERE DINOSAUR
BONES ARE FOUND?

WHERE HAVE YOU TRAVELED?

HAVE YOU EVER WALKED
IN THE SAME AREA WHERE
DINOSAUR TRACKS
ARE FOUND?

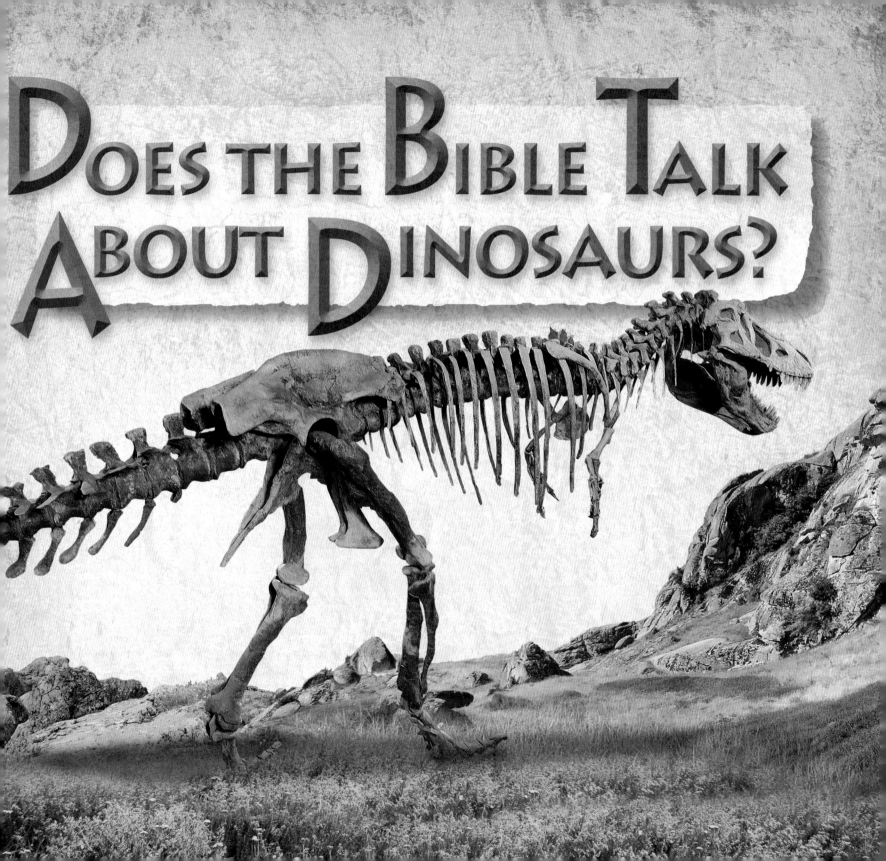

"IF YOU LAY A HAND ON HIM [leviathan],
you will remember the struggle
and never do it again! . . .
"His back has rows of shields tightly sealed. . . .
"A club seems to him but a piece of straw;
he laughs at the rattling of the lance. . . .
"He makes the depths churn . . .
and stirs up the sea" (Job 41:8, 15, 29, 31, NIV).

FIGURE 9.1. Some people think that the whale was the leviathan described in the Bible. *Photo courtesy Dreamstime.com*

Some people think this text from the Bible is talking about a dinosaur. Let's look carefully at the text to see if that's true.

The text says, "He makes the depths churn . . . and stirs up the sea." The animal described here lived in the sea. But as far as we know, dinosaurs lived only on land. So this animal probably wasn't a dinosaur. We don't know what animal the Bible is talking about here. It could have been any large animal that lives in the sea, even a whale.

Here's another Bible text that talks about a very strange animal:

"Look at the behemoth . . .
which feeds on grass like an ox. . . .
"His tail sways like a cedar;
the sinews of his thighs are close-knit. . . .
"Under the lotus plants he lies,
hidden among the reeds in the marsh"

(Job 40:15, 17, 21, NIV).

FIGURE 9.2. Some people think that the hippo is behemoth. *Photo courtesy Dreamstime.com*

Many Christians think this text is talking about the large-bodied dinosaurs. But the text says, "Under the lotus plant he lies . . ." A big dinosaur wouldn't fit under a lotus plant.

Some Christians believe the Bible is referring to a hippopotamus. Others say hippos don't have tails as big as a cedar tree. When you read the Bible, read it carefully. The Bible says that the animal had a tail that "sways like a cedar." It doesn't say the animal's tail was the size of a cedar tree.

Other people think this animal was a crocodile. Remember, the Bible also says the animal ate grass. Can you think of a big animal that lives in shallow water and eats grass?

Some Christians believe that the Flood destroyed the dinosaurs. They think the dinosaurs were too big and too mean to live with people. You've been reading about dinosaurs. You know that about half of the kinds of dinosaurs were the size of a grown-up male giraffe or smaller. You know that they walked around. They ate food. They laid eggs and had babies. What do you think?

"All things bright and beautiful,
All creatures great and small,
All things wise and wonderful,
The Lord God made them all."
—hymn by Cecil Frances Alexander

FIGURE 9.3. About half of the kinds of dinosaurs were the size of a grown-up male giraffe or smaller. *Photo courtesy Dreamstime.com*

WHAT
DO
YOU
THINK?

Happy Hunting

I WROTE THIS BOOK to spark your thinking. I meant it to help you study the wonders of God's creation. Think about the facts as a Christian. Think for yourself about dinosaurs. Read the Bible. Think about your life with God. Look at the world around you. Take time to stop and think about what you see in nature. Know that the design you see shows the great mind of God.

Laugh with God as you watch the animals. Rest with God as you walk. Smell the flowers. Climb the trees. Walk in the mountains. Feel the winds on the plains. Drink lots of water in the deserts. Play in the oceans. Think with God about the world in which the dinosaurs once lived.

In this little book, I've tried to give you good facts about dinosaurs. I don't want to tell you what to believe about dinosaurs. God has given you the gift of a good mind. I think that you can figure out for yourself what these bones mean. Dinosaurs are not a problem for Christians. They were beautiful creations of God. Maybe what I think will help others think too.

In closing, I want to share with you two Bible texts that have guided me through the years:

"Call to me and I will answer you and tell you great and unsearchable things you do not know" (Jeremiah 33:3, NIV).

"I can do everything through him who gives me strength" (Philippians 4:13, NIV).

May God richly bless you as you study His universe!

—Dr. Elaine Graham-Kennedy

PEOPLE TO THANK

Over the years, I've read a number of acknowledgments that list names of people I'll never know. I've often thought that there were some real stories behind those paragraphs, but they were never shared with the reader. I consider those lists to have unfortunate oversights, so my list will be just a bit different.

When I first began my work in geology, I promised myself that I would never write a book, just give lectures. This volume is the culmination of more than fifteen years of lectures. During that time, I received support and encouragement from more people than I can possibly remember. Various comments and bits of information have come from pastors, teachers, and young people over the years, and that has pushed me to dig a little deeper into these issues. Thank you, thank you! There would be no book without your interest in and love for dinosaurs.

I know this is uncommon, but I want to thank God for opening my eyes to the needs of the Christian community with respect to this topic and for giving my previous boss, Dr. Jim Gibson, consummate patience. Many years ago, Dr. Gibson suggested I write a little booklet on the topic, and I faithfully promised to do so each year thereafter. Thanks, Jim, for asking about the book and for waiting without nagging. You are a jewel!

Due to some rather serious illnesses in my family, I've had to cut back on travel and field research. This gave me time to write about dinosaurs, and it is also the time when Tim Lale, Pacific Press acquisitions editor, came into my life. Tim has kids who are "just that age," so his enthusiasm and interest in the book inspired me to do something serious for our young people. Thanks, Tim, for caring about the kids who want to know more about dinosaurs from a Christian perspective.

Tim put me in touch with Jerry D. Thomas, the author of the Detective Zack series and a great children's writer and editor. Thanks, Jerry, for your willingness to help me.

I would also like to thank my former colleagues Ben, Tim, and Raul for their helpful comments, as well as Dr. Lee Spencer, Dr. Roberto Biaggi, and Professor Carlos Steger, who were a tremendous help to me during my research in Patagonia.

Dr. Art Chadwick and I have worked together in the Grand Canyon and eastern Wyoming. He has been a great friend and colleague. Thanks for your review of the book and for all your photos. I know I hounded you to do it when we were both busy on two other papers!

Special thanks go to Tim Standish, who gave me several of his photos for the book. I also need to thank Laurie McMillen Rogers for her photographic assistance at Mesa Southwest Museum, Dr. Lee Spencer for the microscopic photo of an eggshell, and Professor Carlos Steger for the photo of the egg he reconstructed.

A big thank you to the museums and personnel who—although they do not endorse any, most, many, or some of the Christian ideas in this book—allowed public photos: David Rhys Museum, Libertador San Martin, Argentina; Dinosaur National Monument Visitors' Center, Jenson, Utah, <www.nps.gov/dino>; Geoscience Research Institute, Loma Linda, California, <www.grisda.org>; Glen Rose State Park; Korean Nature Conservancy; Mesa Southwest Museum, Mesa, Arizona, <www.cityofmesa.org/swmuseum>; Montana Nature Conservancy, Choteau, Montana; Museum für Naturkunde Berlin, <www.museum.hu-berlin.de>; Natural History Museum of Los Angeles County, Los Angeles, California, <www.nhm.org>; North American Museum of Ancient Life, Thanksgiving Point, Utah, <www.thanksgivingpoint.com/museum>; Southwestern Adventist University Online Fossil Museum, <geology.swau.edu/fossil>; Tyrrell Museum/Alberta Community Development, Drumheller, Canada, <www.tyrrellmuseum.com>.

One can never make a list like this without thanking family. My husband, Dee, has tolerated my eccentric lifestyle as a geologist for too many years, and I thank him for that. Without his loving support, I would still be a college dropout. My precious daughters, Shelley and Ami, have endured long absences while Mom pursued her education and career. Thanks for your patience, for reading an early draft of the book, and for your encouraging feedback. I also want to thank my parents and Dee's parents for believing in me and loving me through all the ups and downs.

There is one last person I need to thank, and that is Mr. Mauk, my ninth-grade biology teacher at Longfellow Junior High School in Enid, Oklahoma. When I turned in my report on Darwin's *On the Origin of Species*, I was somewhat distressed. I've never forgotten his comment on my paper, and I probably never will. (See "About the Author.") I have great sympathy for all of my teachers and colleagues since that time.

God bless you all.

About the Author

Dr. Elaine Graham-Kennedy was born and raised in Oklahoma. She accepted Jesus Christ as her personal Savior at seven years of age, beginning a lifelong walk with God. She loved school and performed well academically but admits she wasn't a valedictorian and didn't consider herself particularly bright. However, she was in a college-bound program and was placed in advanced classes from fourth grade onward.

Because of the advanced placement, she took biology in ninth grade. It was there that she discovered her great love of science. Elaine also discovered a conflict between her personal religious faith and the theories of the Darwinian evolutionists. After reading Darwin's On the *Origin of Species*, she wrote a rather heated paper. Her teacher made a comment on the front of the report: "Elaine, don't let one man's ideas upset you so much." She laughingly admits that she interpreted his comment to mean that she was as smart as anyone else. She decided she should think for herself, making her own decisions about what she believes.

As Elaine continued to study science and entered the field of geology, she was encouraged by teachers and professors to challenge their thinking as well as her own. She loved it! It fed her competitive side very well.

During her high school years, a new pastor came to Elaine's church and told the congregation that their denomination had misunderstood Genesis. He proceeded to explain a perspective on science that he called theistic evolution. Elaine thought these ideas solved all her problems and resolved all her conflicts. However, a new problem arose on her first fossil-hunting trip.

The class drove through eastern Oklahoma, stopping at several places. At one road cut, Elaine worked her way up the hillside, making notes and collecting samples, looking at corals and the shells of clams and snails. Reaching the top of the hill before any of the other students, Elaine sat down and looked across the landscape at the small nearby hills. Then, glancing down, she noticed that she was sitting on gravel. She decided to examine the gravel to see if she could figure out what kind of rocks were in it. At that point, she discovered that the "gravel" topping the hill was a pile of one-celled marine organisms called Foraminifera—animals that create a shell about the size of a wheat seed. According to the geologic record, the animals on that hill had died about three hundred million years ago.

Elaine lifted her hands filled with these little "forams" and watched them run through her fingers like sand on a seashore. Looking up, she realized that these animals topped the hills that surrounded her too, and a question confronted her: What kind of a God do I serve? She couldn't accept the death of millions of organisms before the sin of Adam and Eve in the Garden of Eden. Death before sin was not an option for her theologically.

It wasn't then, and it isn't now. Elaine has spent most of her career helping others understand this issue.

WHY I WROTE THIS BOOK

My editor wanted to know why I would write a book for young people about dinosaurs. Let me start with an analogy. When Christians express their disbelief in evolution by saying, "We didn't evolve from monkeys," they are immediately labeled as being ignorant. That's because scientists don't believe we came from monkeys either! They think that apes (which are not monkeys) and people have a common ancestor that was apelike. But once you say people didn't come from monkeys, scientists assume that you don't know the truth about evolution, and there is no way you can convince them otherwise.

Too many Christians don't know the truth about dinosaurs, so they are ineffective when they talk to people who love dinosaurs. If you want to talk with kids and adults about dinosaurs, you need to know quite a bit about them. This book is filled with dinosaur information and ideas about how dinosaurs fit into the biblical account of earth history. It is filled with good information that you can use. It is written so your kids can read it, but it is also written for you—the parents, grandparents, and mentors of these kids.

As I have lectured on dinosaurs in churches over the years, I have been appalled at the lack of knowledge among members and shocked by their thinking regarding dinosaurs. The Boomer generation in our church has been taught one of two things: (a) the dinosaurs never existed or (b) Satan scattered the bones of the dinosaurs throughout the earth to confuse us. Consequently, young people are confused about what the church believes about dinosaurs.

As I began looking at this problem, I realized that any Christian materials these kids were using to learn about dinosaurs were written by people who were interested in dinosaurs but who didn't know how to separate the data from the interpretations. Or they were reading stuff written by unbelievers. Our publishing houses offer very little on dinosaurs: one volume in the Detective Zack series written some years ago and a little book written by Harold Coffin and Gerald Wheeler for adults. Since my research includes the study of sediments associated with dinosaur materials, I decided that perhaps it was time to make a contribution in this area for our kids, teachers, pastors, and families, both spiritual and natural.

You might think that you don't need to know about dinosaurs. I attended a professional meeting several years ago where teachers heard one speaker say, "We can't take kids who have been raised in a conservative home and convince them in one semester that evolution is true," and another lecturer say, "If we can convince the little kids in kindergarten of two things—one, that dinosaurs lived millions of years ago, and two, dinosaurs evolved into birds—we will have them as evolutionists for the rest of their lives." We have little children in church who already believe those two things. If you attend a church where there are little kids or big kids, you need to know about dinosaurs.

That brings me to another point. Have you seen the Jurassic Park movie trilogy? Most of the kids have. Do you know what is true and what is fantasy in those films? If you answered No to either of those questions, read this book and then rent the films. Watch them by yourself so you can differentiate between the good stuff and the fantasy stuff. Then, watch them with the elementary-school kids in your life who have already seen the movies. Let them know what's fake.

You can say stuff like (my Boomer lingo shows here): "Wow! That is so cool! But no one knows that for sure." "Oooo, that's disgusting, but I don't think anyone really knows how big the piles of dung were." You get the picture, literally and figuratively. This is an important reality check that adults and kids need to do together, even if they are watching a nature show about dinosaurs.

The database for dinosaurs suggests many explanations regarding their appearance in the fossil record, their behavior, and their demise. This book lays out some of the data for several varieties of dinosaurs discovered around the world, and it suggests some possible explanations for a few of the questions raised by the Christian community. Since this book attempts to explain some of the information from the rock record within the context of the biblical record, these explanations will be informed by a variety of biblical concepts held primarily by the conservative, evangelical Christian community.

It is my desire that this book will be received as an honest attempt to suggest some ideas that are both faithful to the scientific data and supportive of biblical beliefs.

In our hearts now and perhaps in the kingdom to come . . .

Vives les dinosaurs!

SCIENCE BOOKS ABOUT DINOSAURS

Please note that these books were not written from the Christian perspective, but they are good books for finding facts. If you look at several, you will soon discover that they do not all agree. New data are found, and theories change.

The Age of Dinosaurs in Russia and Mongolia. M. J. Benton, M. A. Shishkin, D. M. Unwin, and E. N. Kurochkin, eds. Cambridge: Cambridge University Press, 2000.

L. M. Chiappe and L. Dingus. *Walking on Eggs*. New York: Scribner, 2001.

The Complete Dinosaur. J. O. Farlow and M. K. Brett-Surman, eds. Bloomington and Indianapolis: Indiana University Press, 1997.

Dinosaur Eggs and Babies. K. Carpenter, K. F. Hirsch, and J. R. Horner, eds. Cambridge: Cambridge University Press, 2000.

The Dinosauria, 2nd ed. D. B. Weishampel, P. Dodson, and H. Osmólska, eds. Berkeley: University of California Press, 2004.

Encyclopedia of Dinosaurs. P. J. Currie and K. Padian, eds. San Diego: Academic Press, 1997.

M. Lockley and A. P. Hunt. *Dinosaur Tracks and Other Fossil Footprints of the Western United States*. New York: Columbia University Press, 1995.

M. Lockley and C. Meyer. *Dinosaur Tracks and Other Fossil Footprints of Europe*. New York: Columbia University Press, 2000.

J. A. Long. *Dinosaurs of Australia and New Zealand*. Cambridge, Mass.: Harvard University Press, 1998.

D. B. Weishampel and L. Young. *Dinosaurs of the East Coast*. Baltimore: Johns Hopkins University Press, 1996.

How Do You Say It?

Name	Say It	Name	Say It
Allosaurus	AL-oh-sawr-us	Hypsilophodontid	hip-suh-LOAF-oh-don-tid
Archaeopteryx	are-key-OPP-ter-icks	*Iguanodon*	ee-GWAN-oh-don
Brachiosaur	BRAK-ee-oh-sawr	Ornithischian	or-ni-THIS-key-an
Brontosaurus	BRAWN-toe-sawr-us	Ornithopod	or-NITH-oh-pod
Ceratopsian	ser-uh-TOP-see-an	Ossify	AW-si-fy
Chasmosaur	KAS-mow-sawr	Pachycephalosaurid	pack-ee-KEF-uh-low-sawr-id
Coelophysid	see-low-FY-sid	*Pachycephalosaurus*	pack-ee-KEF-uh-low-sawr-us
Coelophysis	see-low-FY-sis	Protoceratopsid	pro-toe-SER-uh-top-sid
Coelurid	see-LURE-id	*Psittacosaurus*	sigh-TACK-oh-sawr-us
Compsognathid	comp-sow-NAY-thid	Saurischian	saw-RIS-key-an
Confuciusornis	con-few-shus-OR-nis	Sauropod	SAWR-oh-pod
Corythosaurus	kor-ITH-oh-sawr-us	Scutellosaurid	SKEW-tel-low-sawr-id
Deinonychus	die-NON-ee-kus	Segnosaur	SEG-no-sawr
Diplodocus	di-PLOD-oh-kus	*Stegosaurus*	STEG-oh-sawr-us
Dromaeosaurid	dro-MAY-oh-sawr-id	Theropod	THER-oh-pod
Dromaeosaur	dro-MAY-oh-sawr	*Triceratops*	try-SER-uh-tops
Epiphysis	e-PI-fy-sis	*Tyrannosaurus*	tie-RAN-no-sawr-us
Fabrosaurid	FAB-row-sawr-id	*Utahraptor*	YOU-taw-rap-tor
Hadrosaurus	HAD-row-sawr-us	*Velociraptor*	vel-AW-seh-rap-tor
Heterodontosaurid	he-tur-oh-DON-toe-sawr-id	*Zuniceratops*	zoo-nee-SER-uh-tops
Homalocephalid	hoe-mal-oh-KEF-uh-lid		